ABOUT THE AUTHOR

The author Fathima Shareef was born in 2008 to Fareeda Gafoor and Shareef Gurukkal. She is studying in eleventh grade at St Teresa's Anglo Indian Higher Secondary School, Kannur. She wishes to bring life to words where humanity, love and peace exists.

Fathima started writing from an early age and was able to publish three poetry collections and now introducing this creation 'Perished in Spring' to the world.

When she's not writing her favorite hobbies includes reading till she's tired of it which she would never and kalari.

English Language
Perished in Spring
(Poems)
by
Fathima Shareef

♦

Published in October 2024
by Kairali Books Private Limited
Thalikkavu Road, Kannur.
Ph : 0497-2761200
E-Mail : kairalibooksknr@gmail.com

♦

Cover Design
Prasanth Mangad

♦

97/24-25/Sl.No.1664/150/NS 18.6
ISBN. 978-93-5973-426-2

PERISHED IN SPRING

FATHIMA SHAREEF

Kairali Books

Dedicated to all the children in war.

Perished in Spring

"Perished in Spring" is a set of fifty poems that brings the true colours of life to existence. In this quickly modifying world, the book captures the beauty and sorrow around. The book expresses the thought that love is simply not a term but is something that needs to be earned. The book contains the poems she wrote for fifty days taking in note everything around.

A note of solidarity

All my life I've always been grateful for having a roof over my head, for not starving , for getting to wear dresses and for having a place to call home.

If it is unusual for you to care for people just kilometers away, you are being blinded by the fragmented treasures of the universe. It is indeed disappointing that now it has become an obligation for people to remind one another and convince them that the slaughtering of an unarmed group of people is a violation of human rights.

Why is it so hard for people to realize that bombing children is unforgivable and that separating family is disgraceful? It is never too late to be on the right side of history.

The Florist of Desires
E.V. Ramakrishnan

Fathima Shareef is a promising poetic talent, still in her teens. She has published three volumes of poems, *The Invisible Gift*, *Zest* and *Sapphire*. The poems of this volume, *Perished in Spring* have to be read against the anguished statement she has given at the beginning of the book, 'A Note of Solidarity'. Here she asks: "Why is it so hard for people to realize that bombing children is unforgivable and that separating family is disgraceful?" This larger awareness of the tragic times we are living in, informs the title and the poems in this volume. The poems are more like diary jottings over a period of six weeks. The everydayness of her transient thoughts is informed by a deeper search for the meaning of love and home in our times.

One of the poems reads like this:

> May 22
> I have lost count of times
> We've said that we care,
> Of times we've been each other's home.
> Would all these feasts rot?
> Would all these seeds perish?
> They say it would.

Love goes with a sense of insecurity and disquiet. Fathima captures this darker side of love convincingly with the word, 'perish' in the above line. She seems to know that the season of spring is not all lush green and full of bird-songs. It can also spell disaster. Her mixed feelings about the rosy side of life shows a growing awareness of the complexity of the world we live in. Home, like love, can be elusive. In the poem titled, 'May 11' she asks: "Are we home?/Are we done running?"

Despite 'the alarmed sea' and 'the unhinged sky' invoking a troubled world, she celebrates the overwhelming nature of love, its power to transform life. These lines capture the momentary feeling of elation and excitement at the meeting of lovers:

> She made her way to him
> Wearing a beige nylon attire
> Being the florist of his desires.

'The florist of his desires' is an arresting image, which shows the elegance her lines are capable of. Not all poems achieve the same lucidity of expression. Maybe it is necessary for her to spend more time revising and rewriting her poems, delving deep into the contours of her emotions, to move beyond the present stage.

Fathima's resolve to listen to her innermost thoughts and feelings, and her concern for the suffering of others are elements that these poems bring out vividly. She has a feel for words, and an eye for details. All this will stand in her stead, as she navigates the perilous slopes of her pains and pleasures of growing up. Let us hope she will realize her full potential as a writer in the years to come.

May 1

For the first time
I felt like I wasn't the poet
But rather a thought
Provoking a young man to love.
For the first time
I felt how it was to be the poem,
To be jotted down in a piece of paper
For the first time,
I felt nothing like myself.

May 2

He does cry
And his eyes do mourn.
His lips do stutter
And his words sometimes concise.

May 3

She was stuck in the labyrinth of desires,
In the snow of December.
Her orbs seems to be wilted and withered
And her limbs as pale as ever.
Her tears swollen from anger
And her fists deceased.

May 4

A lacuna I found
Where your orbs perfectly fit.
I would gladly give in myself
Even in the absence of peace.

May 5

In the midst of growing up
I forgot to be her.
Her smile pale
And her eyes mostly shut.
Her cheeks not flustered as always
And her laugh not soothing enough.

May 6

Amidst the deep ocean
And the dark clouds,
I refused to look back
For all I wish for
Is to be a part of you,
To not be blue and parched.

May 7

He came up to me
And shoved something in my hand.
Muffins I thought it was
Or rather flowers,
Lavenders or maybe orchids
But ink grasped my skin
Or so I thought.
It was you,
Sealed and tied in red.

May 8

Hold my hand
And rub your thumb against it.
Seal a kiss on my forehead
And take me on ice cream dates.
Show up at my door at twelve,
Holding a bouquet of lilacs.
Climb up my window
And tell me you care.

May 9

As he peeked through
He saw her
Between the frosty florist shop.
She made her way to him
Wearing a beige nylon attire
Being the florist of his desires.

May 10

Along the alarmed sea
And the unhinged sky,
Words muttered down my spine
But the sphere held me back.

May 11

Are we home?
Are we done running?
Your lips parted
But they never made a sound.
Are we done loving?
Are we tending to forget?
Your hands lifted
Yet they never shook in denial.

May 12

The thought of her disturbs my sleep.
A touch of her fleecy cardigan
And her tinted smile sprain my eyes.
A part of me wish for her
And a part of me against our regard.

May 13

Do you miss those days?
You and me,
Indie music and lights,
Ball gowns and ties,
Do you?
Do you miss those days?
Carnivals and rides,
Bows and books,
Do you?

May 14

His absence forged
And ferns took over my yard,
As he held me halted.

May 15

Serene, he passed by.
His love spoiled and thrived,
His touch lethal and distracting
And in the midst of knowingness
I fell in the hands of a wallflower.

May 16

Will we ever be sixteen again?
Will we ever listen to each other sing?
We've loved all these days
Would we be able to do so tomorrow?

May 17

Our heart was a pantry of essentials
And yet we weren't asked for.
Our worries were lofty enough
And yet we earned no praise.

May 18

There my fellow mate stood
With a limpid way to life
And there a part of me stood
Trying to unclog the burden.

May 19

I hear nothing but cries of demise
And the sorrow of a widow.
The feeling hold on to me
And I soon became a part of her
And inside,
It was vague and hasty,
Havoc and filthy
And so it was true
That I heard nothing but cries of demise.

May 20

Nothing but foam surrounds me,
Not roses or even seeds.
The peepers seem to not bother anymore
And they say we have departed.

MAY 21

When the flowers refused to grow,
We called them in
For their scents sleeved our hearts.

MAY 22

.

I have lost count of times
We've said that we care,
Of times we've been each other's home.
Would all these feasts rot?
Would all these seeds perish?
They say it would.

May 23

Back in those days,
I'd settle behind you,
Whispering sweet nothings.

May 24

I was drenched in red
Or rather my sweat.
Miles of running from you
Got my knees weak.
The steepest of my joy
And the wrath of my dreams
All remained drenched in red.

May 25

I was obliged to grieve
And a part of me mostly sane.
As I read through their lips,
I collided back down.

May 26

Where lilies fail to find their color,
I loved densely.
Aisles of our footprints
And the stairs of callings before me.

May 27

Every piece of you and me
Collided back into our so called home.
The scent of our ardor and lust
Now nestling beneath our feet.
The smitten letters are now buried down
And our dreams plunged into a sack.
The tantalizing orbs that once held me imprisoned
Soon wilted along with the autumn leaves.

May 28

I write for you
And for the days ahead.
I wish to jot down a part of you
And surrender a part of me.

May 29

I wish to never depart from your arms
And cherish you for long.
I wish to soothe your worries
And cleanse them neat.
I wish to crimson your lips
And whisper words of devotion.

May 30

"Why do we get to see this?
Why stay awake every night?
Why open our eyes starving?
Why leave when I have not grown much?"
Cried out a kid.
Her tears covered pores,
Then came a thud
And she fell still.
Her hopes still remain,
The screams her mother let out
Echoed the walls of their home,
A home that no longer remains.

May 31

The wind blew a little stronger
And the screams a little louder.
Her arm was all I could gather up
And the rest of her lies somewhere unbothered.
Amidst the voices around
I could hear her lips
Chant hymns for survival.

June 1

She stood there unarmed
And yet she remains the same.
Her heart a home to flowers
And her touch mostly lethal.

June 2

"The world is unfair" she said
And I believed, I believed.
I was turning into something
And into someone I don't realize
And yet I believed.

June 3

I have grown nearly as tall as you
And now they all remain a mere thought.
A thought that no longer gets me confused
For I have grown out of it.

June 4

He sneaked in pieces of cakes
And loved her the most.
He took her out for tea
And brought her French robes.
He was an oblivion to everyone but her.

June 5

We sat against the wall
Waiting for us to be called in,
They say we are nothing but immigrants
And that we are still in search of home.

June 6

Between the pile of pansies
And amongst the crowd
I would still lean near your fragrance.

June 7

Handcuffed in the land of their roots
And denied to breathe.
Tightened up in their homes
And asked to survive.

June 8

The lights went out,
It was just you and me
And six hours of tango.

June 9

I watched her be happy
And then saw her head near piled up books.
I saw her admirable orbs
But also her glistening tears.

June 10

There in the sand
Where the sea meets.
I would hold your palms
And make a path between.

June 11

I would rather chase the wind
Than not know our future.
In the midst of growing up,
I found home.

June 12

Her hands felt at ease
And her presence armed.
In those faded blue eyes
I saw the urge to fight.

June 13

I was merely a thought
Or I was rather convinced.
I was a mere thought
And I could never be more.
.

June 14

I came across the strands of your hair
And the nails you bit off
For the thought of you lingers in me.

June 15

The noises woke me up
And baba lay asleep.
Rubbles were right over his legs
And something red beside him.
A year passed by
And baba still lay there
With the rubble over his leg.

.

June 16

In the balcony I sat,
Knitting in a dirty old robe
As I watched the kids play.

June 17

I have grown past my mid thirties
And I have grieved enough.
I have grown past my mid thirties
And I have grieved for the world,
For those lying out there,
And for those near me.

June 18

Beside me I saw you
Or rather a glimpse
Of what you could have been
And when the windows were shut
I saw you
Or rather a glimpse of what you could have been.

June 19

No windows were opened
For that would be a disgrace to the lady.
No blue orbs were alive
For that would be unfair to the mistress.

9 789359 734262